Ancient Greece

KEVIN JANE AND PRISCILLA WOOD

ACKNOWLEDGEMENTS

The authors and publishers would like to thank the following for permission to reproduce photographs and other material:

Alistair Muir	47
Allsport	47
Ashmolean Museum, University of Oxford	cover; 15-17; 19; 21; 23; 33; 37; 39
Bridgeman Art Library	29
The Trustees of the British Museum	7; 9; 13; 15; 19; 22; 23; 27; 28; 32; 38-41
Chris Fairclough	9; 46
Grosvenor Museum, Chester	6
Mary Evans Picture Library	18; 42; 43; 45
Michael Holford	title page; 6; 9; 12; 13; 15; 17-19; 21; 24; 25; 30-32; 35; 36; 38; 39
Paul Walters	cover; 5; 10; 26
Ronald Sheridan/Ancient Art and Architecture Collection	cover; 7; 9; 21; 26; 29; 34; 37; 42- 45
Tate Gallery	47
Thomson Holidays	4; 5; 7; 8; 10; 11; 22; 23; 27; 37; 46

The publishers have made every effort to contact copyright holders but this has not always been possible. If any have been overlooked we will be pleased to make any necessary arrangements.

First published 1993 by Folens Limited, Dunstable and Dublin.
Folens Limited, Albert House, Apex Business Centre, Boscombe Road, Dunstable LU5 4RL, England.

ISBN 1 85276111-3

Cover Design: Hybert Design & Type.
Illustrations: Images in Design, Trevor Parkin.
Printed in Singapore by Craft Print.

CONTENTS

Aghia Marina, the main holiday resort on Aegina.

Aegina offers an ideal holiday ... with a long sandy beach, a relaxed and friendly atmosphere, classical sights and interesting nightlife.

1. Greece Today

Greece is a small country (smaller than the United Kingdom), and you can see from the map that part of it is made up of little islands. Many people who live in the United Kingdom go to these islands for their holidays.

Aegina is one of the most popular Greek islands for holidays. To get to Aegina you can fly to Athens airport, go by bus to the port at Piraeus and then take a ferry to the island.

? A popular island

Look carefully at the information in this unit. It has all been taken from holiday brochures.

1. Find the island of Aegina on the map of Greece.
2. Why do you think Aegina is so popular? Make a list of the reasons.
3. Would you like to go there?

Hotel Apollo

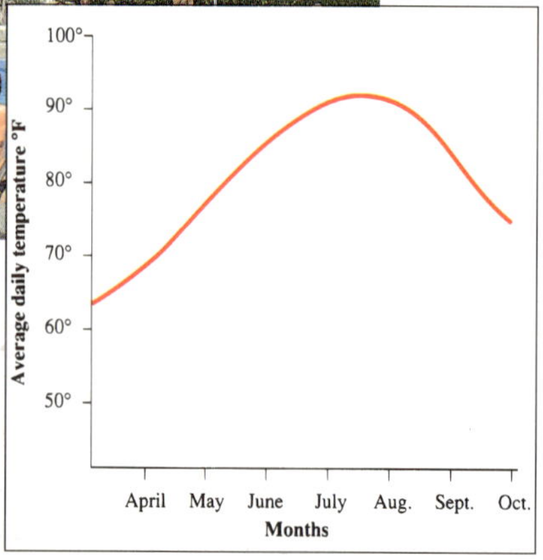

This graph shows the temperature in Aegina during the holiday season.

A travel brochure describes how easy it is to reach other parts of Greece from islands such as Aegina.

Frequent ferries make it easy to spend a hot day exploring Athens and to return in the cool of the evening to an island ... You can (also) take the ordinary inter-island boats and hop to Poros, Hydra and Spetsai.

Holiday plans

Imagine you are going to Aegina for your holiday.

1. What time of year would you like to go?
2. Use the information in this unit to plan how you will spend your time there. Think about where you will stay, what you will see, how you will relax and where you will eat.

The road map of Aghia Marina shows where the main buildings and tavernas are. Tavernas are small restaurants that serve Greek food, usually very cheaply.

The Apollo is one of the hotels in Aghia Marina. As well as offering food and accommodation, it provides table tennis, mini-golf, tennis, a shop, a restaurant and a rooftop pool with sunbeds. The price chart tells you how much it costs to stay at the hotel for one week. The price also covers the flight to Greece.

Road map of Aghia Marina.

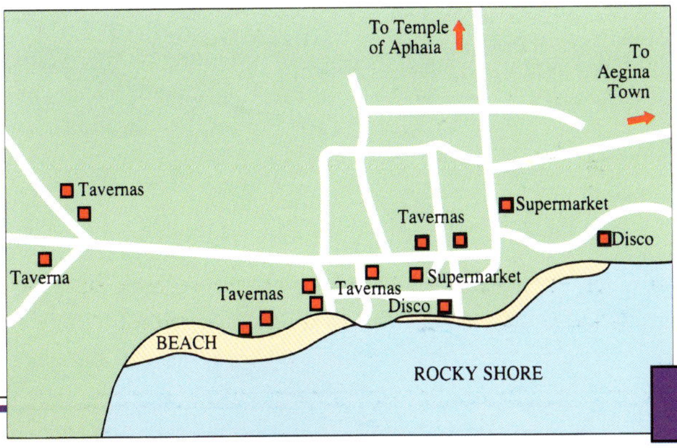

Date	Adult £	Child £
6-30 April	219	159
1-19 May	239	179
20 May - 11 June	245	169
12 June - 9 July	265	189
10 July - 4 Aug	289	198
5-24 Aug	289	198
25 Aug - 10 Sept	279	189
11 Sept - 1 Oct	259	169
2-31 Oct	239	159

Price chart for the Hotel Apollo.

Half the picture

Holiday brochures do not tell us everything about a country. They are advertising things for tourists to do.

1. Do some research to find out how Greeks live in the towns and countryside.

The photograph above shows the Temple of Aphaia. It is a clue as to what you are going to explore in this book. You are going to be historians and try to find out what life was like in Ancient Greece. First, you must journey back in time nearly 3 000 years ....

Future ages will wonder at us, as the present age wonders at us now.

2. When did the Ancient Greeks Live?

AD → 0, 100, 200, 300

BC → 0, 100, 200

The Romans begin their conquest of Ancient Greece.

The time line shows some of the major historical events which took place in Ancient Greece. In this book you will be finding out about daily life during the **Classical Age**.

The State of Sparta founded 900 BC.

900

1000

The Trojan War

1100

1200

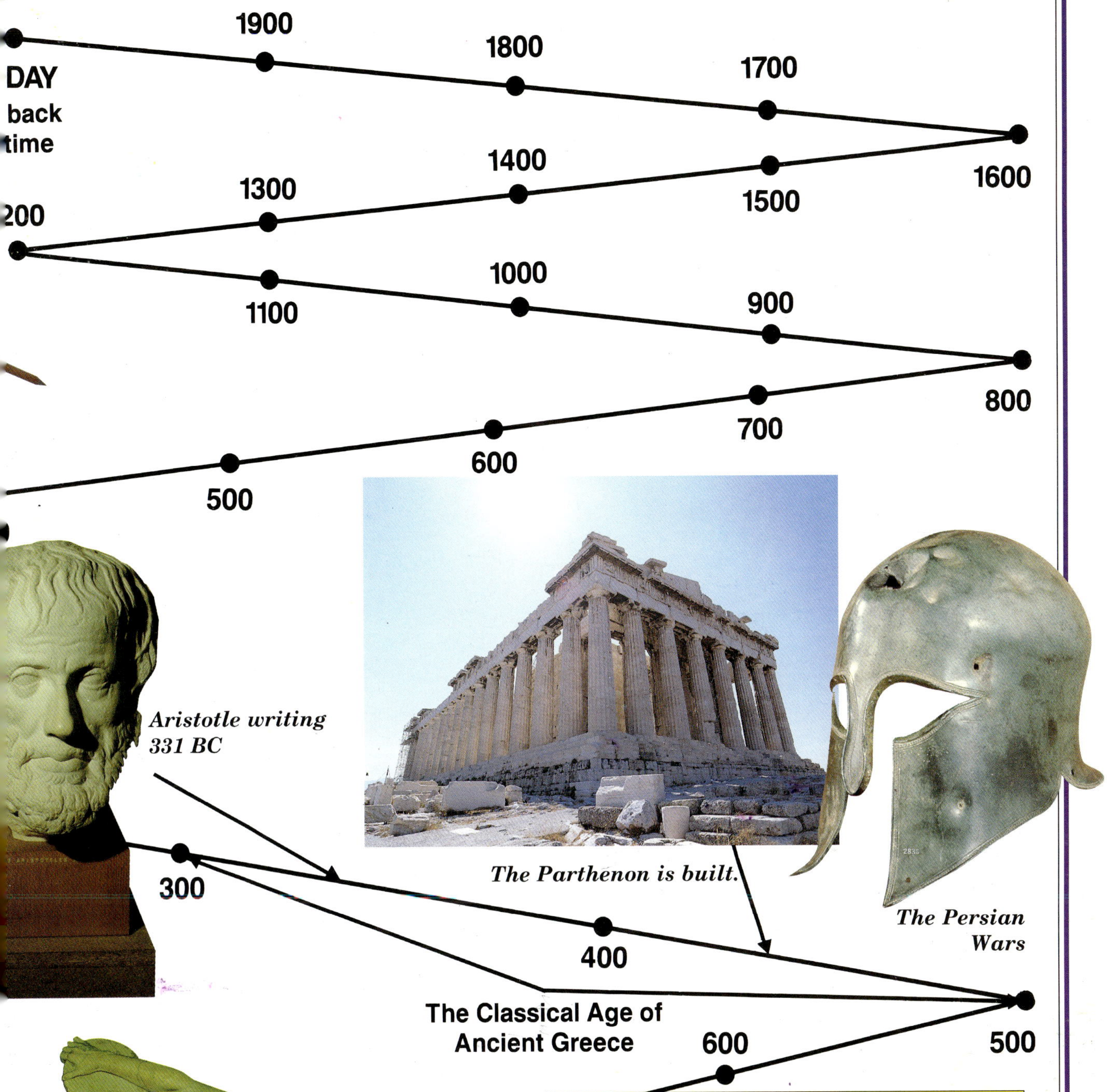

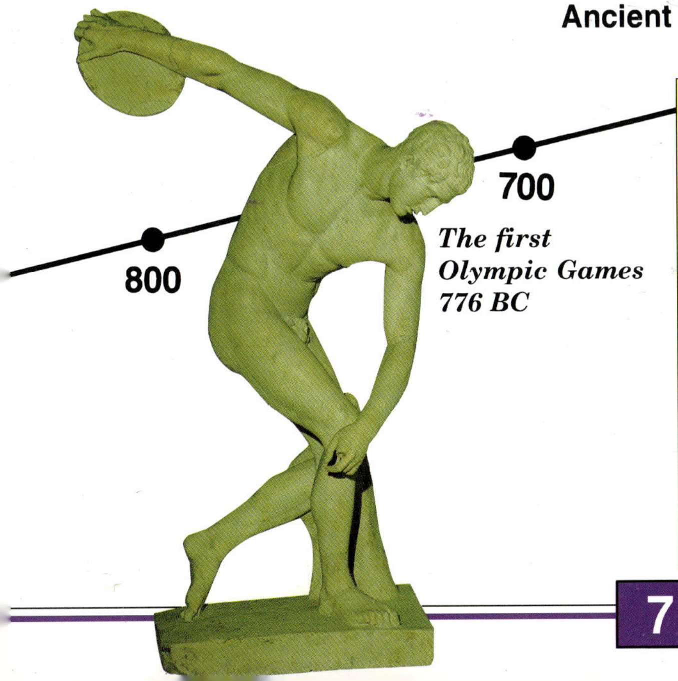

On time

Look carefully at the time line.

1. Working in groups, draw up a big time line like the one above.
2. Mark on as many key events as you can think of which took place between 200 BC and today.
3. Compare your time line with those drawn up by other groups. Have you chosen the same events? Why do you think this is?

Mighty indeed are the marks and monuments ... we have left.

3. How do we know about the Ancient Greeks?

To find out how the Ancient Greeks lived, we need to start by asking questions:

- When did they live?
- What did they look like?
- What work did they do?
- How did they amuse themselves?

? Asking questions

In groups, discuss what you would like to know about the Ancient Greeks.

1. Write down a list of all the questions you want to ask.

To answer these questions you will need to look at **evidence**. Evidence is anything that has survived from the past that helps us to understand what life was like. The Ancient Greeks left behind many different kinds of evidence such as buildings, jewellery, pottery, writing, bones and pictures.

The picture below shows the British Museum in London. Inside there are a huge number of Ancient Greek artefacts. You may not be able to visit the museum yourself, but in this book you will find many photographs of the objects in the museum.

Sir Arthur Evans and Heinrich Schliemann were two famous archaeologists. They discovered many Ancient Greek buildings and artefacts in the nineteenth century.

Heinrich Schliemann (left) and Sir Arthur Evans.

Looking at evidence

Look carefully at the evidence in this unit.

1. Make a list of the ways we can find out about the people who lived in Ancient Greece.
2. What do these sources tell us about the Ancient Greeks?

I win by my strength which is only right and fitting for a Spartan youth.

4. The City States

Ancient Greece was not one country with one ruler. It was made up of many small city states. Each city state (called a *polis* in Greek) had an area of high ground on which a temple was built to honour the city's chosen deity (god or goddess). Below the temple were the people's homes and an open area, called the *agora*, which was used for markets and meetings. A wall enclosed the temple, the surrounding buildings and the *agora*. The countryside outside the walls was used for farming.

Life was different in each city state. Each state had its own laws and government and there was often fighting between the states.

The two most powerful city states were Athens and Sparta. In Sparta two royal kings ruled together with the help of a Council of Elders. The kings' main responsibility was to lead the army. A strong army was very important to the Spartans because they had been defeated in several wars and were determined to keep themselves well defended. This system of royal kings and a council is called an *oligarchy*, meaning "rule by a small group".

Setting the scene

Look carefully at the pictures of the modern Greek landscape in this unit.

1. Prepare a page for a tourist brochure explaining the main features of the modern Greek landscape.
2. Which features of Ancient Greece would have been similar?
3. Which features would have been different?

Sparta became the strongest city state because of its powerful army. Physical fitness, bravery and fighting skills were very important to the Spartans. Boys were taken from their families at the age of seven and trained to fight. Girls also had to keep fit, so that they would produce strong babies. If a newborn baby was weak it was left to die.

Life in Sparta was harsh and uncomfortable. There is little evidence of any art, music, drama or great architecture in Sparta.

A Spartan life

Look up the word "spartan" in a dictionary.

1. What does it mean?
2. How do you think it came to have this meaning?

At one time, about 250 000 people lived in the city of Athens and in the surrounding countryside. The people of Athens were not ruled by kings or queens. Instead the citizens ruled themselves. This system is called a *democracy*, meaning "rule of the people".

In Athens every citizen could vote in the assembly place called the *Pnyx*. Here the laws were discussed and voted on. A council made up of 500 men was selected by lot each year, and it was responsible for the day-to-day running of the state. Women, foreign visitors and slaves could not vote. They were not citizens, so they were not allowed to take part in council meetings.

Comparing lifestyles

Read all the information in this unit about Sparta and Athens.

1. Draw up a table like the one below.
2. Write in the table what you think were some of the good points and bad points of each system.
3. Which city state would you have liked to live in?

	Good points	Bad points
Athens		
Sparta		

Nicias led his army on, and the Syracusans ... pressed them hard in the same way as before, showering missiles and hurling javelins in upon them from every side.

5. The Greeks at War

The army of each city state was made up of trained citizens. In Athens all eighteen-year-old male citizens were given two years of military training. In spring each citizen went to the *agora* to see if he had been chosen to fight that year. Summer was the season for wars between the city states. The wars were fought to gain land, corn, goats and slaves.

Some soldiers fought on horseback. They were not very efficient because they had no saddle or stirrups. The best soldiers were the foot soldiers called *hoplites*. They were called this because each soldier carried a shield called a *hoplon*. They marched close together with their shields in front, to protect themselves.

The Greek city states also fought wars against other countries. For nearly forty years, Athens and other city states were at war with Persia. The Persians were led by King Darius, and then by his son, King Xerxes. They wanted to capture Greek lands. Many battles were fought on land and at sea. Athens was destroyed by the Persians, and had to be rebuilt. Finally, the Greek city states won the long war against the Persians and many Greek writers wrote about what happened.

Armour and weapons

Look carefully at the sources in this unit. They show the weapons and armour of wealthy soldiers.

1. Describe the clothes worn by the Ancient Greeks to protect themselves in battle.
2. What sort of weapons did they use?
3. How do you think the weapons and armour of the poor soldiers differed from those of the rich?

The Greeks often fought at sea, as well as on land. *Triremes* (war galleys) were fast, efficient and easy to handle. They carried crews of up to 200 men.

The playwright, Aeschylus, described the result of a sea-battle:

Many of the Persian ships capsized and we could hardly see the surface of the water for wreckage and drowned sailors. Soon every nearby beach was black with Persian corpses.

Fighting at sea

Look at the vase painting above.

1. Decide which is the *trireme* and which is the merchant ship. (Remember, the merchant ship had to be big enough to carry cargo.)
2. How were the *triremes* powered?
3. Look at the bow (front) of the *trireme* for clues as to how the ship attacked other boats.
4. Read the extract from the play by Aeschylus. What do you think the Greeks tried to do to other ships and why?

Investigations

Use your school library or resource centre.

1. Find out about the following:
   - the Battle of Salamis (a naval battle between the Greeks and Persians)
   - the Battle of Marathon (a land battle between the Athenians and the Persians)
   - The Peloponnesian War (between Athens and Sparta)
   - Alexander the Great.

Foot shields and a helmet.

The inside of a typical house may have looked like this.

The type of house lived in by ... any of the great men of the day ... can be seen to be no grander than its neighbours.

6. Houses

Archaeologists have found the remains of many large public buildings, but very few remains of people's homes. With so little evidence it is difficult to know exactly what a typical Ancient Greek house looked like. The houses were built of sun-dried mud bricks which were laid directly on the earth, without any foundations. Even the houses of rich and important people were very simple.

? The buildings

Most Greek houses were built to house large families. Grandparents, children, aunts, uncles, cousins and slaves all lived together in one building.

1. Why do you think there are so few remains of these houses?
2. Draw a sketch to show how you think these houses may have looked on the outside.

However, there is a lot of evidence to show us what life was like inside Greek homes. Statues and paintings give us clues as to how people cooked, ate, entertained themselves, washed, cleaned their houses and cared for their children.

Household activities

Look carefully at all the sources in this unit.

1. What activities are taking place?
2. In which rooms do you think these activities took place?
3. Make a list of the rooms that each house may have had.
4. Now look at the picture showing the inside of a house. Decide where each room on your list may have been. Explain your decisions.

In a household ... we are most likely to get annoyed with those servants whom we employ to perform the routine tasks.

7. Work in the Home

If we use Ancient Greek art as evidence, we can find out about the type of work carried out in the home.

Finding the evidence

Look carefully at the sources in this unit.

1. Can you find any evidence to suggest that the jobs on your list were done in the home?
2. Record any evidence in the second column of your chart.

Jobs done in the home	Evidence found	Who did the work?
Cooking	Statue	

Household tasks

Draw up a chart like the one below.

1. Discuss all the jobs that you think had to be done in a Greek home.
2. List them in the first column of the chart.

Jobs done in the home	Evidence found	Who did the work?
Cooking		

In Ancient Greece there were free people and slaves. Slaves were owned by rich people and worked as servants in their homes and on their farms. Some slaves were bought from traders, others were captured in war. They often lived and worked closely with the family. Many of the household jobs would have been done by slaves.

Summarise the evidence

Use your chart and the information in this unit.

1. Prepare a written summary about the work done in an Ancient Greek home. Remember to say who did the work and what evidence you found. In your summary you can include jobs that were not on your list, if you have evidence for them.
2. Now present your findings in a different way.

Who did the work?

Look closely at the sources again. Can you tell who is doing the work?

1. Is it a man or a woman?
2. Do you think it is a free person or a slave?
3. Record your decisions in the third column of your chart.

Jobs done in the home	Evidence found	Who did the work?
Cooking	Statue	A woman, maybe a slave

Hence, my excellent friend, you must train the children to their studies in a playful manner and without any aim of constraint.

A modern picture showing what a Spartan school might have been like.

8. Childhood

In Ancient Greece, the father of a newborn baby had to decide whether to let the baby live or die. If a baby looked weak or unhealthy it was left to die. This may seem cruel to us, but remember that there were no hospitals and few medicines in Ancient Greece.

If the father decided that the baby was healthy enough to survive, a special naming ceremony was held. This ceremony was called the *amphidromia*, and it welcomed the child into the family.

Babies and toddlers

Look at the artefact and picture opposite.

1. What do you think each object was used for?
2. Do we use anything similar today?

Celebrating a child

There are many types of celebration to welcome a new baby into its family or community.

1. How many different celebrations can you think of?

In Ancient Greece children were educated to prepare for their adult roles. This meant that boys were educated differently from girls. It also meant that the education varied from state to state.

In Athens, boys were taught basic arithmetic and how to read and write. Many were taught by private tutors, who may have been slaves. Others went to small schools. Some boys also learnt how to play a musical instrument and were trained in athletics.

In Sparta, boys were taught to fight and most of their school time was spent training to be fit and strong. Spartan girls were also sent to school for physical training.

Most Greek girls were taught at home, usually by their mothers. Girls were often married at the age of fifteen. Their husbands were chosen for them by their fathers.

Education for girls

Think about the role of women in the home (see unit 7).

1. What skills did girls need to learn to prepare them for their adult lives?
2. How does a girl's education today differ from that in Ancient Greece?
3. Are there any similarities?

Can you identify these Ancient Greek toys? Do children today have similar toys?

Here you are, take this yellow gown and put it on.

9. Clothes

Chiton

Fashion in Ancient Greece did not change as quickly as it does today. Clothes were made by hand and the designs were very simple. They did not need complicated cutting or much stitching.

The most common garments were the *peplos*, the *chiton* and the *himation*.

Himation

Peplos

Most clothes were made from wool which was spun and woven at home. Linen was also popular but it had to be brought from places such as Egypt. This made it more expensive than wool. Cotton was not grown by the Ancient Greeks so cotton clothes were rare and also very expensive.

Most vase paintings show people barefoot. The scent bottle below is shaped like a foot in a sandal. It gives us a clue as to what some Ancient Greeks wore on their feet.

Hairstyles

Most Greek women had long hair.

1. Using the evidence in this unit, sketch some of the Ancient Greek hairstyles.
2. What do you notice about how the men wore their hair?

Footwear

Footwear was rarely shown in Ancient Greek art.

1. Can you find any examples of footwear on vase paintings or statues in this book?
2. Is there anything like the sandal above?

Identifying types of dress

Look at the pictures in this unit.

1. Which types of dress are these people wearing?
2. Which garments do you think were worn mostly by women?
3. Which were worn mostly by men?

I used to be a farmer - the sweetest life on earth ... bursting with honey-bees, bloated with sheep and olives.

10. Food and Agriculture

Greece is a very mountainous country and only about one fifth of the land can be used for farming. However, in Ancient Greece most of the people earned their living by farming. The soil was poor and hard. Wet winters followed by long, hot, dry summers meant that few crops grew. It was difficult to grow enough grass for the animals to eat.

By reading Ancient Greek poems, plays and essays we can find out about what people grew and the animals they kept. Pictures on domestic objects, such as vases and cups, also provide us with evidence.

A Greek poet, Moschus, described a fisherman's life:

A wretched life a fisherman's must be,
His home a ship, his labour in the sea,
And fish, the slippery object of his gain.

A farmer's life

Look at the information in this unit.

1. Do you think that a farmer's life was "the sweetest life on earth"?
2. What evidence have you used to make your decision?
3. Describe what a farmer's life might have been like.

Gathering olives from a tree.

Some Greek writers described the farming life:

... here is the season for shearing your sheep of their spring wool.

I feed a thousand sheep, and from them drink excellent milk; and never want for cheese.

The earth smelled of rich summer and autumn fruit: we were ankle-deep in pears, and apples rolled all about our toes. With dark damson plums the young sapling branches trailed on the ground.

A woman baking bread.

A bronze statue of a farmer ploughing.

A modern historian describes the diet of the Ancient Greeks:

... stone-ground bread, goat's cheese, a handful of olives and figs, diluted wine, a little honey, some eggs and dried fish, with meat a rarity to be eaten only on feast days ... or some other special occasion.

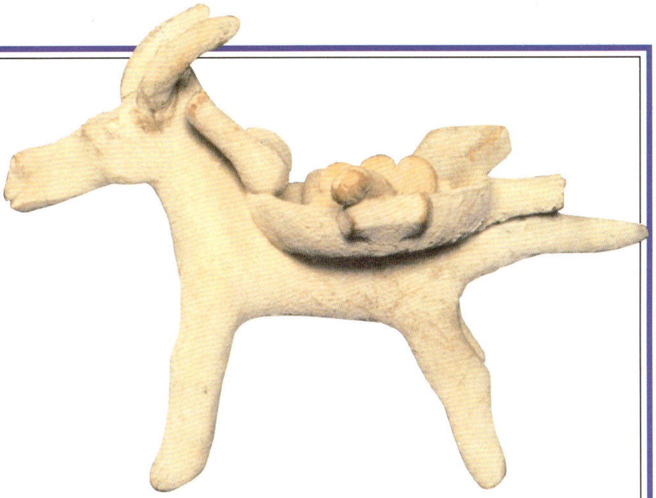

The basket on this terracotta mule contains fruit (probably figs), cake, a cheese-grater and a pestle and mortar.

The diet

Read the modern historian's description of the Ancient Greek diet.

1. What evidence confirms this was the usual diet?
2. Can you suggest anything else that might have been eaten?

Farming today

Look at the pictures of modern farming in Greece. In some ways farming has not changed very much from ancient times.

1. How do you think a modern farmer's life is different from a farmer's life 2 500 years ago?
2. What are the reasons for these differences?

The best time to go sailing is July or August. You won't wreck your ship or drown your sailors then.

11. Trade and Sea Transport

The Ancient Greeks could not grow all the crops or produce all the materials that they needed. The landscape and climate were good for growing grapevines and olive trees, but the land was too mountainous to grow enough wheat for the people.

Bread was one of the basic foods for most Greeks, so large amounts of grain had to be imported. Merchants sailed all over the world to buy grain and other goods which the Greeks were unable to produce themselves.

Trading ships

The painting on the vase above shows an Ancient Greek trading ship.

1. Look at the painting and then draw your own picture.
2. Record how the ship was powered, steered and where the cargo might have been kept.
3. Why do you think an eye was painted on the bow of the ship?

Imports

Look carefully at the map below. It shows which countries traded with Ancient Greece.

1. List the places which supplied Greece with grain.
2. What other goods were imported and where did they come from?

Travel

Look at the map of Greece and the pictures of the Greek landscape in unit four.

1. Why do you think travelling over land may have been difficult in Ancient Greece?
2. Why did sea travel become very important?

Money

Look at the photographs of Ancient Greek coins.

1. Compare them with modern coins. How are they similar?
2. How are they different?
3. How do you think they might have been made?
4. Compare this method with modern coin-making.

The Ancient Greeks exported pots, statues, oil and wine. In early times there was no money and the Greeks swapped these goods for other things that they needed.

The first place to use money was a wealthy state near Greece, called Lydia. The Lydians used flat discs of solid silver and gold to trade for basic goods such as food and wine.

The architectural beauty they created in sacred buildings and their adornment was of a quality and an extent unsurpassable by later generations.

12. Great Buildings

Although little remains of Ancient Greek houses (see unit 6), the ruins of some public buildings still stand today. These buildings were made from hard, strong materials, such as marble and limestone. The stones were fixed together with metal bolts and pegs. The buildings were strong enough to withstand thousands of years of weathering.

Identifying the buildings

Look carefully at the two pictures on this page.

1. Which do you think is:
   - the Theatre of Dionysus?
   - the Temple of Aphaia?
2. Think of words to describe these buildings.

What can you see in these carvings?

Let us take a closer look at the remains of one public building. The picture below shows the Parthenon in Athens. It was a temple built in honour of the goddess Athena.

The Ancient Greeks were very proud of their public buildings and they spent a great deal of time, money and energy building them. The Parthenon took fifteen years to build.

The design of the Parthenon was simple. A line of elegant columns ran round the outside of the building, supporting lintels. These lintels were decorated with stone carvings. At each end of the building the lintels were topped with stone triangles called pediments.

There were many different architectural styles in Ancient Greece. The Parthenon was designed in the Doric style. This meant that the capitals were plain and the columns sturdy and undecorated at the base.

In the Inner Temple, a continuous, carved frieze ran round the top of the building. These carvings were of fantastic creatures, deities and heroes from Greek myths and legends. They are now known as the Elgin Marbles.

The Elgin Marbles were named after the Earl of Elgin who lived in the eighteenth century. His name was Thomas Bruce, and when he visited Greece he was greatly impressed by the beauty of the Parthenon. The ruins were crumbling so Elgin decided to make drawings and plaster casts of the carvings. Then he started to collect pieces of the frieze and had them shipped back to Britain.

These statues and carvings are now in the British Museum in London, but there has been a lot of discussion about whether they should stay in Britain or be sent back to Greece.

? The Elgin Marbles

The Elgin Marbles are of great historical and artistic value.

1. Do you think that Thomas Bruce was right to bring pieces of the Parthenon to Britain in the 18th Century?
2. Do you think the carvings really belong to the British or the Greeks?
3. What do you think should happen to the collection now?

The gods know, and we call upon the gods; they know how we are spun in circles like seafarers, in what storms.

13. Beliefs

Zeus, the king of the Olympian deities.

The Ancient Greeks believed in many deities. They believed that the twelve most important deities were all part of one family who lived on the top of a great mountain called Mount Olympus. These twelve deities were called the Olympians.

There is a large amount of evidence about the Olympian deities. Temples were built in their honour. Statues of them were made for people to worship, and Greek stories and plays are full of tales about them.

A model of the Temple of Zeus at Olympia.

The statue below is of Aphrodite (called Venus by the Romans), the goddess of love and beauty. The statue is called the Venus de Milo and can be found in the Louvre Museum in Paris. It is probably the most famous statue from Ancient Greece in the world today.

The Greek gods and goddesses were believed to be immortal (have everlasting life), but in other ways they were like humans. For example, they could fall in love, argue, be happy, angry, sad and jealous.

The Greeks told many stories about their deities and used them to explain things in the natural world which they did not understand.

One of the most famous myths is about Pluto, the god of the Underworld. He fell in love and kidnapped Persephone, daughter of Demeter. Demeter was goddess of all plants, and when Persephone was kidnapped she neglected her plants to search for her daughter. This caused winter. Eventually, Persephone was allowed to return to her mother for six months of every year, bringing spring and summer with her.

? The role of the deities

Each of the Olympian deities had a special responsibility in the world.

1. Read the four extracts below. They are all taken from Greek plays. Decide who was:
   - the god of the sea
   - the god of music
   - the goddess of hunting and the moon
   - the god of the weather.

*"Artemis,
Daughter of Zeus and huntress,
Queen of shades,
Guiding the light in darkness ... "*

*"Listen, Apollo, you who can wake to song
The seven strings of your lifeless lyre,
Till they chant immortal music to lonely shepherds ..."*

*"Zeus, you sovereign of thunder,
Shiver him with lightning."*

*"Come, dread Poseidon, ruler of the salty oceans;
Forsake thy deep hiding-places
In the fish-filled, frenzied sea."*

A 15th Century painting of the birth of Aphrodite.

Venus de Milo

"That cannot be," said cunning Polydectes, "unless you bring me the Gorgon's head!"
"That I will!" shouted Perseus. "I'll bring it, or die in the attempt!"

14. Myths and Legends

Helios

Look at the vase painting. It illustrates the myth of Helios, who drove his chariot of the sun across the sky from east to west every day.

1. What did this myth try to explain?
2. We use the word "heliosis" today. Look it up in a dictionary and explain where the word comes from.

The Ancient Greeks loved to tell and listen to stories. Some of the stories were connected to religious beliefs and these stories are called myths. They explained things in the natural world, such as the seasons, earthquakes and thunder. Myths also explained what angered or pleased the deities.

Some Ancient Greek stories were based on real events and people. These are called legends.

One famous legend is about Oedipus, a prince of Thebes. Oedipus was adopted at birth, and when he grew up he unknowingly killed his father and married his mother. When he discovered what he had done he blinded himself and fled from Thebes.

Most of the stories were told rather than read. We still know some of the stories today because after many years they were written down. Sometimes they were written as poems, and sometimes as plays.

Homer wrote two epics (very long poems) called the *Odyssey* and the *Iliad*. The *Odyssey* tells the story of Odysseus and his adventures as he returns home after fighting in the Trojan War. The painting below shows one of his adventures.

Orestes killing Aegisthus.

Find out about myths and legends

Below is a list of some famous Greek myths and legends.

1. Find out about these stories:
   - Theseus and the Minotaur
   - Helen of Troy
   - Jason and the Argonauts
   - King Midas
   - Narcissus.
2. Which of these stories do you think are myths and which are legends?
3. Chose a dramatic scene from one of these stories and draw a picture of it.

Theseus and his deeds.

Aeschylus wrote three plays which tell the tragic legend of King Agamemnon and his family. King Agamemnon was killed in his bath by his wife Clytemnestra. Years later, their son Orestes, killed Clytemnestra and her new husband, Aegisthus. The plays tell of these murders and of what happened to the family afterwards.

According to Greek legend, Theseus was the son of Aegus, king of Athens. He performed many brave deeds. He killed the Minotaur, a fierce monster who lived in a maze called the labyrinth in Crete.

Many of the stories described fantastic creatures. Medusa was a gorgon. She had wings, bronze claws, bulging eyes, a protruding tongue, and serpents instead of hair. If anyone looked at her, they turned into stone! The two pictures below show how different artists imagined she looked.

Fables were another type of story told in Ancient Greece. A fable is a short story which has a moral, or lesson to be learnt from it. This one was written by a man called Aesop:

A wolf thought that by disguising himself he could get plenty to eat. He put on a sheepskin to trick the shepherd and joined the flock grazing on the hillside.

At nightfall, the shepherd shut him in with the sheep in the fold and made fast all round by blocking the entrance. Then, feeling hungry, he picked up a knife and slaughtered an animal for his supper. It happened to be the wolf.

A case of mistaken identity

Read Aesop's fable. It is thought that Aesop was a slave who wrote down well-known fables. The morals of many fables are still relevant today.

1. What lesson can be learnt from the fable of the wolf who pretended to be a sheep?

Fantastic creatures

Read the descriptions below.

Scylla
A female with six heads and a ring of snarling dogs around her waist.

Chimaera
A creature with the body of a goat, the neck of a snake, the head of a lion and the tail of a serpent. It breathed fire.

Cyclops
A bad-tempered giant with just one eye, placed in the middle of its forehead.

Sirens
Very beautiful female creatures with lovely voices and bird-like bodies. They were wicked and destructive.

1. Draw a picture of each of these creatures.
2. Compare your drawings with those of your friends.
3. Why are they different?

Two sphinxes on a vase.

Can you see the satyr (with a tail) on this vase painting?

Satyrs and sphinxes

Look carefully at the pictures on this page.

1. How would you describe:
   - a satyr?
   - a sphinx?
2. Do you think they were good or evil creatures? Why?

Comparing myths and legends

Find out about myths and legends from other societies in the past.

1. Can you see any similarities between them and the Ancient Greek stories?
2. What are the main differences?

And some enjoy horses and wrestling, or table games and the lyre ...

15. Leisure

This vase painting shows Achilles and Ajax playing a game. What game do you think it may have been?

How do people spend their leisure today?

Think what people do with their leisure today.

1. Interview some adults to get as many ideas as possible.
2. Decide whether most of the activities are done alone, with one other person, or with a group.
3. Draw up a chart like the one below and fill it in.

Activity	Alone	With one person	With a group
Tennis Dancing			

People in Ancient Greece also enjoyed their leisure. In this unit you can see some of the ways in which they spent their free time.

Dinner parties were very popular among men. It was a time for them to meet, talk and enjoy good food. They were served by their slaves. Wives were not invited to these parties, but the men paid women dancers to come and entertain them. Often at their parties, the men made up poems and riddles, listened to musicians, or watched acrobats.

Musicians, dancers and acrobats were hired to entertain men at dinner parties.

Music was very important to some of the Ancient Greeks. The sons and daughters of rich citizens were usually taught how to play an instrument. We do not know how Greek music sounded because very little written music has been found.

A theatrical scene.

The Greeks loved to tell and listen to stories. Poetry was also very popular. Poems were recited at festivals and parties by men called rhapsodies.

The Greeks also enjoyed going to the theatre to see plays. You can find out more about Ancient Greek plays in the next unit.

Entertainment for the rich and poor

Some of the leisure activities in this unit were only enjoyed by wealthy people.

1. Which activities could have been enjoyed by everyone?

How did the Ancient Greeks spend their leisure?

Look at all the sources in this unit and the next.

1. Draw up a chart to show all the different activities and decide whether they were done alone, with one other person, or in a group.
2. Compare your chart with the one drawn up about modern activities. Are there any similarities? Why are some activities different?
3. Which Ancient Greek activity would you have enjoyed?

Judge our play by its wit and wisdom ... Judge us by the fun we've given you. That should ensure top marks from almost all of you.

This vase painting shows a scene from a comic play. Can you work out what is happening?

16. Going to the Theatre

Going to the theatre was a very important part of Ancient Greek life. Many theatres were built and hundreds of plays were performed.

There were many famous dramatists (people who wrote plays), such as Euripides, Aeschylus, Sophocles (who wrote tragedies), and Aristophanes (who wrote comedies). Tragedies were serious plays which told well-known stories of kings and queens, heroes and heroines. The comedies were usually very up-to-date. They often made fun of famous politicians or other dramatists.

In Athens plays were written for a festival in honour of the god Dionysus. People went to the festival to watch four or five plays at a time. Judges had to decide which play was the best.

Sophocles

? Lost plays

Many plays were written in Ancient Greece, but most have been lost.

1. Why do you think this is?
   (Clue: think about what the plays might have been written on and the number of copies probably made of each play.)

Layout of the theatre

Look at the photograph of the theatre of Dionysus.

1. Discuss and decide:
   - where the audience sat
   - where the actors acted the play
   - why the theatre was shaped as it was
   - where the judges sat.

The theatre of Dionysus in Athens.

There were only a few actors who played the main parts in a Greek play. They often had to play more than one part. There was also a chorus of actors who spoke and moved together.

The actors were always men, so they had to play female roles as well as male roles. Large masks were worn to show which character they were playing.

Masks

Look at the pictures of the masks. They were usually caricatures (exaggerated pictures) of the characters.

1. Why do you think the masks were so exaggerated and so large?

Theatre masks reconstructed to look like the original ones used in Ancient Greece.

Plays written in Ancient Greece are still performed today. They have been translated into many languages so they can be performed all over the world. People still laugh at the jokes in the comedies and are still fascinated by the terrible stories told in the tragedies.

Models of comic actors.

Then, at the sound of the bronze trumpet, off they started - all shouting to their horses and urging them on with their reins.

17. The Olympic Games

In Ancient Greece athletics was one of the most popular sports for men because it kept them fit. This meant that they would be in a good condition to fight if war broke out.

The Olympic Games was one of four major sporting events which attracted competitors from all over the Greek world. These games were held every four years at Olympia in honour of the god Zeus. They lasted for five days. Messengers travelled to all the major Greek cities to announce the Games and all the wars had to end to allow the athletes to travel to Olympia in safety.

Buildings for the Olympic Games

Special buildings were built at Olympia for the Games. Look carefully at the picture below which shows how they might have looked.

1. Decide which buildings were:
   - the Temple of Zeus
   - the stadium for running races
   - the gymnasium.

A model of the Ancient Olympic buildings.

The events

We can see evidence on vases of the kind of events which took place.

1. Look at the pictures in this unit and identify the different events.
2. Do we have the same events in the modern Olympic Games?

Women were not allowed to take part in the Olympic Games. They held their own games at Olympia in honour of Hera, Zeus' wife. There was only one event. What do you think it was, judging by the statue below?

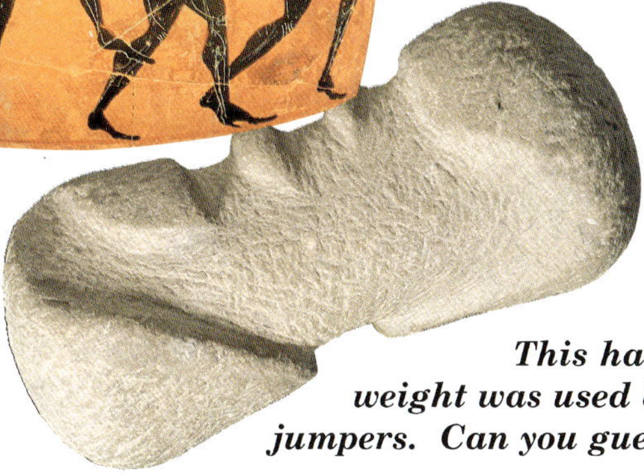

This hand-held weight was used by long-jumpers. Can you guess why?

It was considered an honour simply to compete in the Games. Individual winners were presented with olive wreaths, palm branches or ribbons.

The last Ancient Olympic Games was held about 1 600 years ago. Earthquakes and floods then destroyed the site of Olympia. It was not until the last century that archaeologists discovered the site. In 1896, the first modern Olympic Games was held in Athens.

Literacy, the ability to read and write, has long been one of the hallmarks of civilisation.

18. Language and Writing

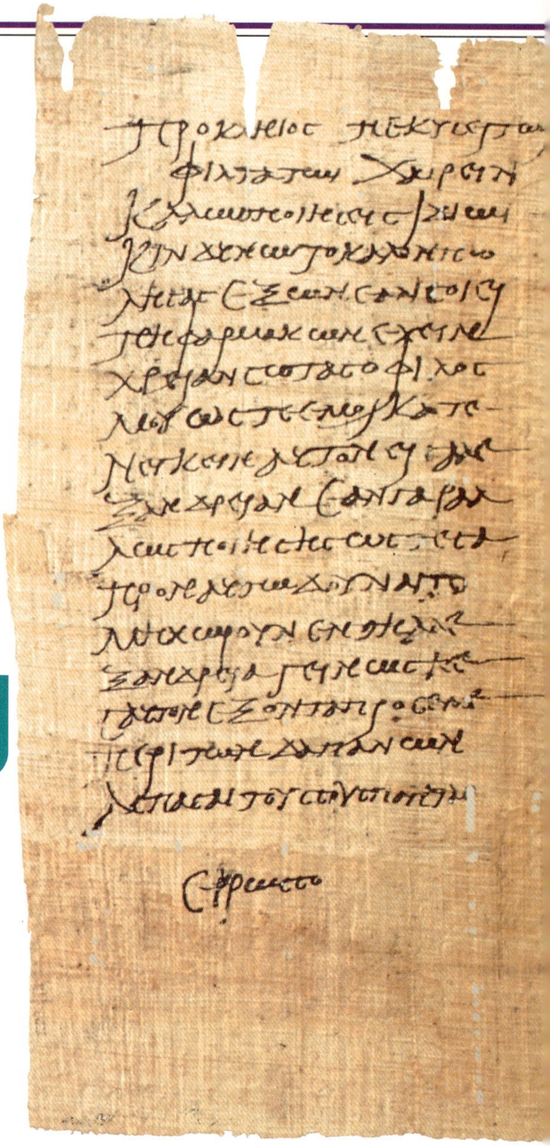

Here is a letter written in Greek on papyrus.

The time before people began to write is called prehistory. The only way we can find out about prehistoric times is by looking at the remains of buildings and artefacts. This makes it difficult for historians to get detailed information about life during these times.

The Ancient Greeks began to read and write very early on in their civilisation. This means that we can use what they wrote as evidence of their lives and way of thinking.

Some of the work of the great writers has survived, but most of it has been lost. The Ancient Greeks did not write, print and publish books to sell to lots of people as we do today. Instead, they wrote everything by hand. There were usually just a few copies of each piece of work. They were probably written on papyrus, which is a type of paper made from reeds.

? The great writers

Here are the names of some of the great writers:

Homer Aristophanes
Herodotus Plato.

1. Look at units 14, 16 and 19 to find out what each of them wrote.
2. What do you think might have happened to the work that didn't survive?

As well as writing great plays and poems, the Ancient Greeks used writing in their everyday lives. Ivory pens were used to scratch words on wax tablets.

Some people wrote down the great tales which had been passed down from generation to generation through story telling. Others wrote down what they had learnt about history, mathematics and science.

Examining the evidence

Wax tablets were useful for writing on because they could be used over and over again. The flat end of pens could smooth over the wax once the writing was no longer needed.

1. What sort of people do you think wrote with pens and wax tablets?
   (Clue: read the extract by Herodas.)
2. What might they have been writing?
3. Who else may have found wax tablets useful?

In a poem by Herodas, a mother complained about her son to his schoolmaster.

His slighted writing tablet,
Which every month I take to wax,
Is left to be forgotten against the wall
Under his bed ... unless he scowls in rage
As though it were his death and
Scrapes it bare instead of writing upon it.

Comparing alphabets

Look carefully at the examples of Greek writing.

1. Make a copy of all the letters that are like English letters.
2. Can you find any letters that are completely different to those in the English alphabet?

The Ancient Greeks also used marble and bronze to write on. They were generally used to record public messages, laws, lists of winners in competitions and so on. These plaques could be hung up in public places such as the *agora*.

This inscription is part of an agreement between Athens and another city state.

When we read things that the Ancient Greeks wrote, we are usually reading a translation. The Greek alphabet is not the same as our alphabet, although many of our letters come from it. The word "alphabet" comes from the Greek words "alpha" and "beta".

Many English words derive (come from) Ancient Greek ones, for example:

- geography
- history
- telephone
- microscope
- hypodermic.

Can you find any more?

19. The Philosophers

Herodotus

Archimedes

In the early years of Greek civilisation, people believed that the deities were responsible for everything that happened in the world. They were thought to control natural things, such as the weather and earthquakes, as well as the lives of people. The past was explained by myths which were part of the religious beliefs of the time.

However, as time went on, many people began to look for more logical and practical explanations for things which happened in the world around them. People also began to record their thoughts and discoveries. These people are known as philosophers, which means "lovers of knowledge".

The Ancient Greek philosophers studied many different subjects and developed ideas and ways of working that we still use today. Some of the greatest thinkers in Ancient Greece are featured in this unit.

Herodotus was an historian. He found out about the past by travelling to places where important events had taken place. He asked people what they had seen and heard. Herodotus is known as "the father of history". In Greek, "historie" means "to learn or know by questioning".

Archimedes invented a system for irrigating and draining land. The system is known as "Archimedes' Screw".

Hippocrates

Euclid

Hippocrates was a doctor. He was one of the first doctors to believe that illness has natural causes. Hippocrates also wrote about how doctors should behave towards their patients.

Here are some of Hippocrates' observations and advice:

Should one part of the body be hotter or colder than the rest, disease is present in that part.

Cold is bad for the bones, teeth, nerves, brain and the spinal cord: heat is good for these structures.

Milk is not recommended for those who suffer from headaches.

Those who are bald do not suffer from varicose veins.

Anaximander was interested in how the universe began. He believed that humans had developed from another kind of animal, possibly a fish or dolphin.

Euclid was a mathematician. He introduced ideas such as an angle in geometry.

? A doctor's opinion

Read the statements made by Hippocrates.

1. Which points do you think modern doctors would agree with?
2. Which points do you think modern doctors would disagree with?

? Our ancestors

Anaximander believed that humans had evolved (developed) over a long period of time.

1. This theory was re-stated by Charles Darwin in Victorian Britain. Find out what the public's reaction was in the 19th Century.

Aristotle is one of the most famous philosophers and among his many projects, he invented a system for classifying animals and plants.

Aristotle

Plato was a pupil of Socrates. He had many ideas about how an ideal state should be run.

Plato

Anaxagoras believed that the sun was a flaming mass and that the moon's light was reflected from the sun.

It is said that Aristarchus believed that the earth turned on its axis and that it moved around the sun. We cannot be sure that this is true, because Aristarchus never wrote his ideas down.

Judging the evidence

Look at the portraits in this unit.

1. Which do you think were done in Ancient Greek times?
2. How can you tell?

Pythagoras worked out ideas in mathematics. His theory about triangles is quite complicated, but it is still used today.

Pythagoras' Theorem

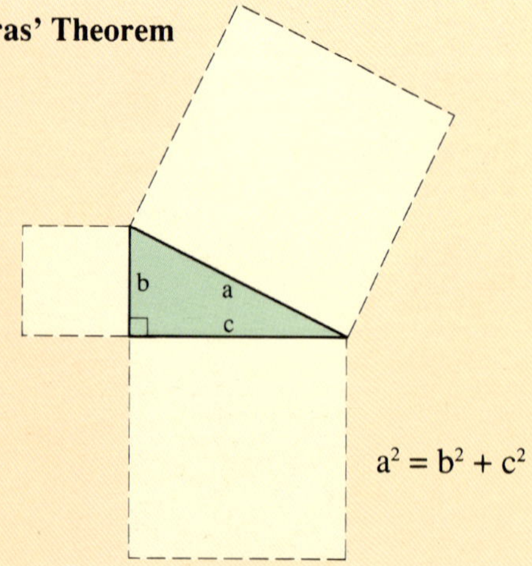

Thucydides was an Athenian historian who wrote about the Peloponnesian War. He served as a general during the war.

Thucydides

? Ideas new and old

Look through the ideas expressed by the philosophers in this unit.

1. Which ideas do we still believe in today?
2. Have any ideas developed or changed?
3. Choose two of the philosophers on these pages and find out more about what they wrote and said.

Socrates was a philosopher who often questioned other people's beliefs. He was unpopular with the politicians of Athens and was eventually sentenced to death.

Socrates in prison, surrounded by his followers.

The Greeks have influenced Western Society more, and more fundamentally, than any other nation known to history.

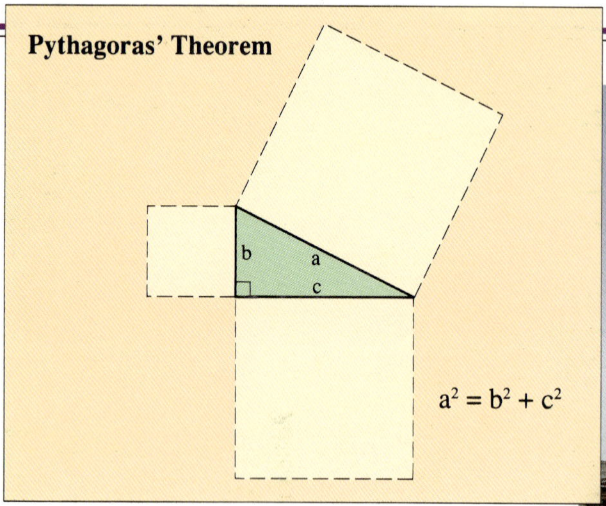

20. The Legacy of Ancient Greece

During the first century BC, the Roman army invaded Greece and made it part of the Roman Empire. The Romans were impressed by many Greek ideas and they copied them. They stole statues, pots and other works of art from houses and temples and took them back to Italy. They also captured Greek people to be slaves and to help teach their children. This helped to spread Greek ideas to other parts of the world.

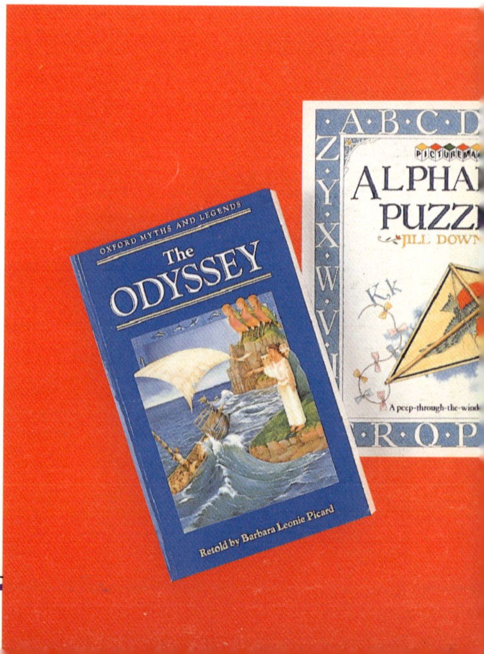

Although the Ancient Greeks lived 2 500 years ago, and on the other side of Europe, their civilisation still influences us today. It is not only western Europe, but nations all over the world who have benefited from the legacy of Ancient Greece.

Look up these words in a dictionary to find out where they come from:

- hypodermic
- polygon
- telescope
- microcosm.

Connecting past and present

Look at the boxes in this unit. Each shows a connection between our world and the Ancient Greek world.

1. Discuss the connection in each picture. You may find it helpful to look back through the book to remind yourself of some of the things you have learnt.

Index